Contents

Summer is the season that follows spring.

The Seasons

Summer

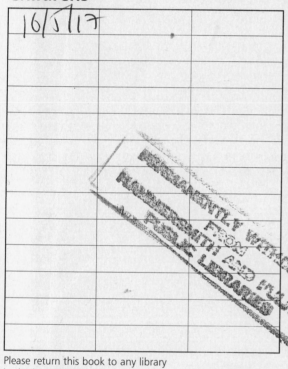

Paul Humphrey

W
FRANKLIN WATTS
LONDON • SYDNEY

First published in 2007 by
Franklin Watts

© 2007 Franklin Watts

Franklin Watts
338 Euston Road
London NW1 3BH

Franklin Watts Australia
Level 17/207 Kent Street
Sydney, NSW 2000

A CIP catalogue record for this book is available from the British Library

Dewey classification number: 578.4'3

ISBN: 978 0 7496 7163 1

Planning and production by Discovery Books Limited
Editors: Paul Humphrey, Rebecca Hunter
Designer: Jemima Lumley

Photo credits: CFW Images/EASI-Images/Ed Parker: 21; Chris Fairclough:
cover pictures, title page, 6, 7 bottom, 8, 10 top, 14, 15, 16, 17, 19, 20, 23, 24, 26,
28, 29 (thanks to Penn Hall School, Wolverhampton); FLPA: 11 (David
Hosking), 12 top (Pete Oxford/Minden Pictures), 12 bottom (Malcolm Schuyl),
27 (David Hosking); Rebecca Hunter: 7 top, 25; Istockphoto.com: 10 bottom
(Arlindo Silva), 13 (Gary K Smith), 18 (Tony Tremblay); Photodisc: 22

Printed in China

Franklin Watts is a division of Hachette Children's Books,
an Hachette Livre UK company.

In summer the weather is usually warm and sunny.

We can go swimming outdoors and eat lots of summer fruits.

Parks and gardens are full of flowers.

The trees are covered with leaves. They shade us from the sun.

There are insects
everywhere.

The birds have plenty
of food to eat.

The tadpoles in the
pond turn into frogs.

Caterpillars change
into butterflies.

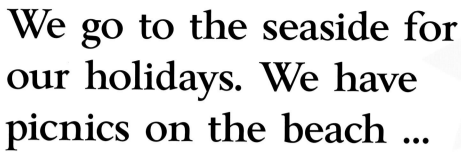

We go to the seaside for our holidays. We have picnics on the beach ...

... and eat ice cream!

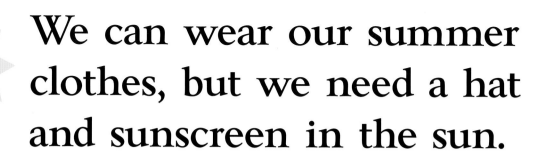

We can wear our summer clothes, but we need a hat and sunscreen in the sun.

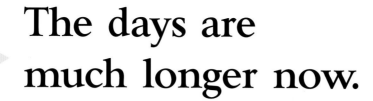

The days are much longer now.

We can play outside
in the evenings.

In mid-summer it often gets very dry.

Rivers and ponds can dry up.

Farmers have to water the crops.

 # Summer storms bring thunder and lightning.

Sometimes rainbows
appear in the sky.

 # Late in the summer, the wheat turns golden brown.

It is time
for farmers
to harvest
the crops.

By the end of summer, the leaves start to turn brown.

Autumn is coming!

Summer projects

Make a butterfly mobile

Caterpillars change into butterflies in the summer.
You can make this colourful butterfly mobile.

You will need:
Some white card ✳ Different coloured felt-tip pens
A wire coat hanger ✳ A needle and cotton thread
Crêpe paper ✳ Scissors ✳ Sticky tape

What to do:
1. Cut out 6-8 butterfly shapes.
2. Colour the bodies of the butterflies in
   brown or black and use bright
   colours for the wings.
3. Wrap the crêpe paper
   around the hanger and
   stick with sticky tape.

4. Thread the cotton through the
heads of the butterflies and tie the
butterflies to the hanger as shown.
5. Hang up your mobile.

Make a frog

By early summer, spring tadpoles are starting to turn into frogs.
Here's how to make a colourful frog.

You will need:
Light green, dark green and yellow coloured card
Scissors ✳ Felt-tip pens ✳ Glue or a stapler

What to do:
1. Cut a semi-circle of dark green card about
30 cm in diameter.
2. Fold the card into a cone shape
as shown, and glue or staple it together.
This is the frog's body.
3. Cut two front and two back
legs from light green card.
4. Cut a round face from
light green card.

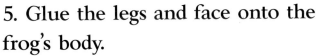

5. Glue the legs and face onto the
frog's body.
6. Cut two small circles from the
yellow card and colour them in
to make the eyes.
7. Glue the eyes onto your frog's
face. Draw on its nose and mouth.
Your frog is finished!

Index